MY LITTLE

URBAN POETRY

No. 1

Haley McHashtag

MY LITTLE URBAN POETRY NO. 1

First edition. March 30, 2023.

Written by Haley McHashtag.

CONTENT

OH, THE THRILL OF STUDENT LOANS

To embark upon a voyage so grand,
The halls of learning, where knowledge stands,
With eager hearts, we pledge our troth,
To the siren call of student loans' growth.

Oh, what joy to sign one's name,
To the binding scroll, a debtor's claim,
A pact with fate, a lifelong bond,
To interest rates that grow beyond.

The years roll on, we toil and strive,
Our future mortgaged, our dreams contrived,
With every paycheck, we offer our due,
The debt collector's grasp, unyielding and true.

At last, we weep, our dreams now stalled,
The weight of debt, our spirits mauled,
For the thrill of student loans, a cruel jest,
An albatross 'round the neck, a lifelong quest

THE SUBLIME JOY OF A BROKEN IPHONE SCREEN

Oh, wondrous moment of pure delight,
When shattered glass meets fingertips' light,
The iPhone, once pristine, now marred,
Its visage cracked, its beauty scarred.

How fortunate are we who bear,
The spiderwebs of chaos, an artful snare,
A canvas of destruction, a testament to fate,
The screen protector, alas, too little, too late.

With every swipe, a thrill, a shiver,
As jagged edges cut and quiver,
A reminder of the mortal truth,
That all things beautiful, must lose their youth.

Rejoice, for in this bittersweet state,
We find solace in our shared heartache,
For in the fractured glass, we truly glean,
The sublime joy of a broken iPhone screen.

The Great American Food Pyramid Heist

Gather 'round, my friends, and hear this tale,
Of a gastronomic crime, a dietary fail,
The Food Pyramid Heist, a caper so grand,
In the land of the free and fast food stands.

Once upon a time, a scheme was hatched,
To subvert our plates, our meals mismatched,
The fruits and veggies, cast aside,
For greasy fries and burgers supersized.

The culprits sly, a corporate band,
Their sights set on the pyramid's land,
With tempting ads, and sugar-coated lies,
They stole the base, oh, what a prize!

And so, we feasted, our wills deceived,
On sugary sodas and processed treats,
The pyramid crumbled, our waistlines grew,
The thieves rejoiced, their profits too.

But all's not lost, for in the rubble,
A glimmer of hope, a nutritious bubble,
The pyramid's spirit, though shaken and scarred,
Awaits a hero, to heal and safeguard.

So heed this tale, and mind your plate,
Defend the pyramid, before it's too late,
Together we'll foil the great heist's reign,
And restore balance to the food chain.

Behold the charmed lives, so dazzling, so bright,
On screens aglow with artificial light,
The Insta-perfect world, a carousel,
Of filtered smiles and tales we tell.

Oh, wondrous façade, so polished and fair,
A thousand likes, a million cares,
The sunsets captured, the brunches shared,
But dare we glimpse the truth laid bare?

Beneath the glossy veneer, we find,
The hidden struggles of heart and mind,
The sleepless nights, the silent tears,
The doubts and fears of unspoken years.

For in the race to curate our lives,
We lose ourselves in the digital tides,
The endless scroll, a siren's call,
To be more, do more, never fall.

So pause, dear friends, and take a breath,

To see beyond the Insta-depth,

For life's true beauty lies untold,

In unfiltered moments, raw and bold.

THE ART OF PROCRASTINATION: A SONNET

In praise of sloth, let me sing the glory,
Of putting off the tasks we find so boring,
The art of procrastination, sweet refrain,
A dance we do to keep our minds untamed.

To while away the hours in idle thought,
And find distractions, as our deadlines fought,
A cup of coffee, just a scroll or two,
The siren call of YouTube, oh, how we rue.

Yet as the clock ticks on, we find our muse,
In panic's grip, the looming hour we choose,
To buckle down and face the dreaded toil,
With frenzied hands, the midnight oil we boil.

And so, we toast to this, our hallowed art,
Procrastination, a game for the faint of heart,
A dance, a duel, a lover's sweet embrace,
A skill honed well, to win the endless race.

CAFFEINE, MY EVERLASTING MUSE

Oh, Caffeine, thou art my muse eternal,
A potent elixir, a love infernal,
With every sip, my heart doth race,
As bleary eyes meet morning's embrace.

In coffee's warmth or soda's fizz,
Thy wondrous powers do not miss,
To rouse the weary, the dreary, the glum,
To thy boundless energy we succumb.

By day, by night, thy charms we seek,
The deadlines met, the goals to eke,
And yet, this love affair, a price we pay,
In jittered nerves and sleep delayed.

But still, we cling to thy dear embrace,
The bittersweet allure, we cannot replace,
Oh, Caffeine, our muse, our savior, our vice,
To the land of the wakeful, you entice.

Oh, the kiss of a fool, a paradox sweet,
A clumsy encounter, when two lips meet,
A bumbling dance, a heartfelt blunder,
A moment of folly, a passionate plunder.

In graceless attempts, to express our desire,
We fumble and stumble, as flames ignite fire,
The ardor's sincere, though technique may lack,
A tender misstep, a loving setback.

Yet, in this clumsy exchange, a treasure we find,
A lesson in love, of the unrefined,
For perfection's a myth, a construct untrue,
In the art of romance, we're all but fools too.

So, embrace the folly, the awkward, the raw,
For in the kiss of a fool, a beauty we saw,
A reminder of our shared humanity,
Oh, the kiss of a fool, an ode to sincerity.

I Won't Teach You a Thing, You Imbecile

I won't teach you a thing, you imbecile,
No wisdom shared, no truths to unveil,
For I am but a youth, what do I know,
Of life's grand mysteries, its ebb and flow?

Yet in my naivete, a spark resides,
A fire untamed, a youthful pride,
I need not lecture, nor condescend,
To share my thoughts, or hearts to mend.

For in the spirit of the young and bold,
A truth more potent than the ancient, old,
A fearless drive to challenge and resist,
The status quo, the ironclad fist.

So, imbecile, heed my words and see,
No lessons taught, but truth set free,
For in the voice of youth, a power unleashed,
A force to change the world, to say the least.

FOMO: A Tragic Ballad

Gather 'round and hear the tale,
Of FOMO's grip, a tragic wail,
The Fear of Missing Out, a curse,
Upon our lives, an endless thirst.

In days of old, we knew not this plague,
But now our screens, a window stage,
To witness others living large,
While we observe, our hearts at charge.

We see the parties, the laughter, the cheer,
And wonder why we are not there,
The envy stirs, a potent brew,
Of longing, yearning, feeling blue.

Yet, in this ballad, a truth's revealed,
The images we see, a falsehood sealed,
For all we witness, a mere display,
Of curated joy, a masquerade.

So, sing with me, this tragic song,
Of FOMO's hold, relentless, strong,
And let us strive to break the chains,
To live our lives, free from these reins.

You Wish to See Me Bare?

You wish to see me bare, unveiled and true,
A brazen request, but I see through,
Your shallow craving, your desire's aim,
To strip me down, objectify my frame.

But I, my friend, am more than skin and bone,
A tapestry of thoughts, of dreams, my own,
I'll not be reduced to a fleeting glance,
A captured moment, a transient dance.

For I am fire, I am the stormy sea,
A force untamed, a spirit wild and free,
My worth, my value, not for you to claim,
I'll not be boxed, or shackled by your game.

So hold your tongue, and curb your appetite,
For I, my friend, will shine my own light,
A mystery, a riddle, a poem unsung,
You wish to see me bare? The night is young.

Unbearable Lightness of Being Unemployed

Oh, the sweet release, the joy untold,
Of days unfettered, no chains to hold,
The blissful state of being unemployed,
A carefree life, so gleefully enjoyed.

No morning rush, no coffee to go,
Just endless hours, a languid flow,
The sun rises, the moon shines bright,
Our schedule's clear, no tasks in sight.

But hark, what's this? A shadow looms,
A creeping dread, that boredom dooms,
The days once cherished, now wear thin,
As purpose wanes, and doubt sets in.

The freedom sought, a double-edged blade,
For idle hands, a price is paid,
The unbearable lightness, now we see,
Of being jobless, is not all it's cracked to be.

In shadows cast, the darkness grows,
A void of purpose, a life in throes,
The state of being unemployed, despair,
The crushing weight of hope, threadbare.

The days stretch on, a monotonous haze,
A fruitless search, a fruitless maze,
The sun may rise, the moon descend,
Yet no reprieve, no journey's end.

In quiet moments, the whispers start,
The doubts, the fears that tear apart,
The questions gnaw, the torment swells,
In this limbo of existence, an empty shell.

Each passing day, a battle waged,
The fight to stay afloat, engaged,
The unbearable lightness, a cruel deceit,
For in this plight, no solace we meet.

But in the depths of darkest night,
A glimmer of hope, a flickering light,
For even in the grasp of the unemployed,
The strength to rise, to soar, unalloyed.

You Think You're So Clever, Nerd

You think you're so clever, a genius, a sage,
A master of knowledge, oh, what a stage,
With your glasses perched high and your books piled tall
You conquer the world, or so you enthral.

But I, my dear friend, must burst your grand bubble,
For life is a mess, a chaotic jumble,
No theorem or formula, no scholarly art,
Can capture the nuance of life's beating heart.

So, strut and preen, in your ivory tower,
While we mere mortals, seek solace and power,
In laughter and love, in the world's great unknown,
Embrace the chaos, the uncharted zone.

For wisdom, true wisdom, lies not in our books,
But in life's messy corners, its crannies and nooks,
So put down your pen, and join us outside,
The world's ripe for learning, a boundless, wild ride.

Oh, sing the praises of a Netflix binge,
A siren call, our wills to unhinge,
The hours lost in endless streaming seas,
A voyage of leisure, of mindless ease.

With popcorn cradled and remote in hand,
We journey forth to digital wonderland,
The dramas, comedies, and thrillers await,
To sweep us away, our fates to abate.

We laugh, we cry, we gasp, we swoon,
As countless episodes, our evenings consume,
The sun may rise, the moon may wane,
Yet still we watch, caught in the streaming chain.

But heed, dear friend, the cost we pay,
As life slips by, our dreams delayed,
For in this vortex of pixelated pleasure,
We lose ourselves, our untapped treasure.

So, break the spell, and step outside,
The world awaits, its arms open wide,
The unstoppable temptation, resist, we must,
To live a life of meaning, free from digital lust.

Hush now, Elon Musk, your fortune vast,
A wealth unmeasured, a shadow cast,
Upon our humble lives, our meager means,
Your rockets soaring, while we chase dreams.

Oh, how you dazzle with your grand designs,
A world transformed, the stars aligned,
Yet we, mere mortals, down on Earth we dwell,
In awe, or envy, it's hard to tell.

But spare us now, your billionaire's grin,
Your Mars-bound missions, your electric din,
For in our hearts, a truth we hold,
That riches, true riches, can't be bought or sold.

So carry on, and chase the sky,
Invent and innovate, let ambition fly,
But hush now, Elon, your wealth we dismiss,
For life's true meaning lies in more than this.

FOREVER YOUNG: THE FEAR OF ADULTING

A specter looms, a darkness near,
The passage of time, a truth severe,
From youth to age, a dreaded shift,
A chasm to cross, an unbridged rift.

The fear of adulting, a haunting refrain,
A burden we bear, a heartrending strain,
With trepidation, we confront the tide,
Uncertain and weary, with nowhere to hide.

In the wake of responsibility, dreams may fade,
As freedom wanes, replaced by a trade,
Of bills and taxes, and endless toil,
The once-fertile soil of youth, now spoil.

We look to the past, a nostalgic haze,
A yearning for innocence, for simpler days,
When hope was abundant, and laughter carefree,
Forever young, a wishful decree.

But the march of time is relentless, it's true,
And adulting's fear, a shadow we must construe,
For in its embrace, we find our path,
To navigate life, its sorrows and its wrath.

The Glorious Struggle of Waking Up Early

Sing the praises of the morning's call,
The battle waged 'gainst slumber's thrall,
The glorious struggle of waking up early,
A test of wills, a journey most surly.

The shrill alarm, our nemesis true,
A siren's song, a torturous cue,
With bleary eyes and heavy heart,
We rise, unwilling, a groggy start.

In darkness still, we stumble, we fall,
Our bodies protest, a lumbering crawl,
Yet, in this fumbling, a comedy we find,
The human condition, a dance unrefined.

For who among us has not known,
The sweet embrace of sleep, overthrown,
By the demands of life, its ceaseless grind,
A tale of woe, to which we're resigned.

So, laugh we must, at our shared plight,
The glorious struggle, from dusk till light,
For in this jest, a camaraderie we share,
The triumph of waking, a badge we wear.

THE DIVINE INTERVENTION OF THE INTERNET

Oh, hallelujah, let us rejoice,
For the Internet, our saving voice,
A gift from above, or so it seems,
A divine invention, the stuff of dreams.

From cat videos to endless memes,
A digital world that truly teems,
With knowledge, folly, and laughter too,
A cornucopia of wonders, to amuse and woo.

We bow our heads, our screens aglow,
In sacred reverence, a techno-show,
The Google gods, we do beseech,
To grant us wisdom, within our reach.

And lo, the WiFi, our lifeline, our tether,
A beacon of hope, in fair or foul weather,
We worship its signal, its bars of might,
Connecting us all, both day and night.

The divine intervention of the Internet, behold,

A modern miracle, a story untold,

Yet in this jest, a truth we find,

The power to unite, the whole of mankind.

You Want a Glimpse, You Fool?

You want a glimpse, you fool, you jest,
Of flesh exposed, my dignity divest,
But who, dear sir, do you think I am,
A trinket, a bauble, a prize to be clammed?

Oh, laughable, the sheer audacity,
To think me prey, your prize fantasy,
But I, my friend, am no mere plaything,
A queen, a force, a tempest, a zing.

My worth lies not in skin, but soul,
A heart ablaze, a spirit untold,
You seek to own, to grasp, to claim,
But I will not be tamed, no shackles, no chain.

So take your foolish, crass desire,
And toss it aside, let it expire,
For I am more than you'll ever perceive,
A mystery, a riddle, a force to be believed.

To the War Veteran

My dear war veteran, to you I bow,
In solemn respect, our gratitude endows,
Your sacrifice, your valor, we cannot repay,
The cost of freedom, a debt we weigh.

In fields of battle, you did stand,
A guardian, a shield, for our cherished land,
Through fire and fury, your courage held,
A testament of fortitude, a story to be retelled.

Your wounds we see, both seen and unseen,
The scars of war, etched deep within,
We honor your pain, your silent fight,
A constant reminder, day and night.

As the years pass by, and memories fade,
We pledge to remember, the price you paid,
For in your struggles, a beacon we find,
A call to action, to be loving and kind.

To the war veteran, we offer our hand,
In unity and support, together we'll stand,
For in your journey, we all must partake,
To foster peace, and a world to remake.

As we look ahead, the future unsure,
We venture forth, our steps demure,
In tentative tones, our voices sing,
A cautious ode, a whispering.

We weigh the options, and consider the cost,
A myriad of choices, a sea to be crossed,
In quiet reflection, we search our soul,
To find our way, to reach our goal.

The path may twist, and shadows loom,
Yet in our hearts, a light we groom,
For even in doubt, and moments of strife,
We cling to hope, the essence of life.

In tender verses, we etch our fears,
A balm for wounds, a solace for tears,
For in this verse, a truth we share,
The strength to face life, to love and to care.

In hesitant whispers, we'll find our way,

Through the darkest night, to the brightest day,

For in our journey, a lesson learned,

That in the face of uncertainty, our courage is earned.

THE LAMENT OF A LOST AIRPOD

Oh, woe is me, a tragedy befalls,
A single AirPod, lost to the halls,
Of time, of space, or between couch cushions,
A lament for the ages, our hearts it worsens.

How could it be, this tiny plight,
Could bring such sorrow, such endless night,
To think of tunes, half-heard, forlorn,
A symphony fractured, a melody torn.

What cruel fate, to steal away,
One half of a pair, a duo astray,
The right, it plays, but left, where art thou?
Our music, our joy, now incomplete somehow.

Alas, dear AirPod, we mourn your demise,
A wireless wonder, now severed ties,
Yet in this farce, a truth we glean,
That life's absurdities can make us keen.

So, laugh we must, at our silly woes,
The trivial troubles, life's ebb and flows,
For in this lament, a lesson we find,
To take life lightly, and leave woes behind.

THE PLACES YOU'LL GO... IN TRAFFIC

Oh, the places you'll go, my dear, my friend,
In a sea of red lights, a journey without end,
The world of traffic, a dance most slow,
A meandering river, a ceaseless flow.

From honking horns to muttered sighs,
A symphony of impatience, the time flies,
But fret not, my comrade, for in this crawl,
A chance to ponder, to muse, to stall.

Look out the window, at life's parade,
The bustling streets, a grand cavalcade,
Each car a story, a tale untold,
Of dreams and fears, of young and old.

In traffic's embrace, we find our peace,
A moment's respite, a subtle release,
For in the stillness, a truth we glean,
That life's journey is but a fleeting scene.

So, smile, my friend, as we inch along,
Our paths entwined, a shared song,
For in this dance of traffic's woes,
We find our kinship, a bond that grows.

The Tragedy of Unread Text Messages

Oh, gather 'round, dear friends, and hear,
A tale of woe, a tragedy most severe,
Unread text messages, the bane of our age,
A Shakespearean drama, upon our digital stage.

In pixelated purgatory, these messages reside,
A graveyard of sentiments, a tomb for our pride,
Our very souls we've poured, into these fading lines,
Only to be left unread, such a cruel paradigm.

The hours, they tick by, yet our screens stay forlorn,
In a cruel twist of fate, our hearts are left torn,
For how can we bear such a weight on our chest,
To send out our love, and receive naught but unrest?

Oh, the scorn of a phone, that relentless device,
With the power to leave us cold as ice,
Could it be that our worth is measured by this,
A read receipt, an emoji, a digital abyss?

How tragic, indeed, this tale we weave,

A world where texts unread make us grieve,

But alas, my friends, in this melodrama we dwell,

No silver lining to offer, no comforting spell.

My Dearest Darling, Spotlight's Queen

Oh, my darling diva, the center of all gaze,
In the classroom's spotlight, you set hearts ablaze,
A vision of grandeur, you prance and you preen,
The epitome of grace, our beloved drama queen.

You flutter your lashes, your smile so beguiling,
As if your mere presence is cause for such smiling,
A narcissus in bloom, your reflection adored,
For who could resist your charm, ever so forward?

Your designer attire, a testament to your taste,
Not a single hair out of place, not a moment to waste,
For the world is your stage, and you play the lead role,
Captivating and enchanting, the queen of the stroll.

But, oh, my dear, as you sashay through the hall,
Have you ever considered the meaning of it all?
In your quest for attention, your parade of acclaim,
Do you find satisfaction, or is it just a hollow game?

Yet fear not, sweet darling, for in this sarcastic verse,
A moment of reflection, a chance to converse,
About the follies of vanity, the cost of pride,
And the truth that lies deeper, beneath the glossy outside.

BLESSED ARROGANCE, BOTH HANDSOME AND DUMB

Oh, you radiant fool, both beautiful and dim,
A walking paradox, a riddle wrapped in whim,
With a smile so dazzling, a visage so fair,
Yet, alas, my dear friend, there's not much upstairs.

A Greek god incarnate, Adonis reborn,
But when it comes to smarts, you've been sadly forsworn,
A case of nature's cruel trick, a terrible jest,
To gift such a face, yet leave the brain underdressed.

You strut through the world, a peacock in plume,
Unaware of your follies, the impending doom,
For though your looks may charm, and hearts may swoon,
It's a hollow existence, an empty perfume.

Yet, worry not, dear simpleton, for in this verse,
A moment to ponder, a chance to reverse,
The fates that have bound you, so handsome and daft,
A blessing and curse, your beauty and lack of craft.

For in this poetic tease, a lesson we share,
That the world's more than looks, more than vanity's glare,
A balance of substance, of wit and of grace,
A journey to wisdom, that all can embrace.

Oh, what a tale, a fable so grand,
Of a sly roadrunner and coyote so bland,
A story of cunning, of wit and of guile,
A desert dance, an endless trial.

Behold the roadrunner, a creature so sleek,
With feathers like lightning, and a beak that could speak,
It dashes and dodges, a master of the chase,
As if life were a game, a marathon race.

And there, in pursuit, the coyote so dim,
A haphazard hunter, with chances so slim,
He schemes and he plots, but to no avail,
His efforts in vain, his plans doomed to fail.

With each cunning trap, the coyote's disgrace,
The roadrunner's laughter, a slap to his face,
For in this eternal struggle, a lesson so clear,
That wit trumps brute force, in this desert frontier.

So, let us all gather, and witness the show,

A comedic ballet, a classic tableau,

Of the sly roadrunner, and coyote so daft,

A testament to folly, a reason to laugh.

THE GLORIOUS TOONS OF AMERICA'S GLEE

In a land where cartoons reign supreme,
A parade of animated shows, an endless stream,
Gather 'round, dear friends, and lend me your ear,
For the American classics, their praises I'll cheer.

First, The Simpsons, a family so bright,
Yellow-skinned and wacky, a satirical delight,
And Family Guy, with crude jokes galore,
A mishmash of gags, a comedic uproar.

Then, SpongeBob SquarePants, that sea-dwelling buffoon,
With his pineapple home, and his pet snail's tune,
And Avatar: The Last Airbender, a tale of might,
A quest for balance, a heroic fight.

Let's not forget Rick and Morty, a duo so strange,
A mad scientist and grandson, through dimensions they range,
And Adventure Time, in the Land of Ooo,
A whimsical journey, where friendships accrue.

As we delve deeper, into this animated abyss,
More American treasures, we simply can't miss,
A smorgasbord of delight, a feast for the eyes,
These wondrous cartoons, a delectable surprise.

Next, we have South Park, with its razor-sharp wit,
No topic too sacred, no stone left unhit,
And the zany Looney Tunes, a nostalgic treat,
Where Bugs Bunny and Daffy, in chaos, do meet.

Behold Gravity Falls, a mysterious land,
With secrets and puzzles, cryptic and grand,
And BoJack Horseman, that melancholic steed,
A show that explores the depths of human need.

Steven Universe, with its cosmic display,
A young hero's journey, a gem-studded foray,
And Regular Show, a slice of the bizarre,
Where talking animals, their adventures do star.

And so, we conclude, this animated spree,
A sarcastic ode to American TV,
These cartoons, these gems, our beloved creations,
A legacy of laughter, spanning generations.

Come one, come all, to this wondrous array,
Of American series, celebrated and gay,
In the realm of TV, where drama and laughter
Intertwine and enthrall, from the floor to the rafter.

First, we have Friends, that iconic display,
Of six charming souls, in New York they did play,
And Breaking Bad, a tale of crime and deceit,
Where chemistry and meth, in chaos, do meet.

Then, Game of Thrones, a saga so vast,
A whirlwind of intrigue, a medieval blast,
And The Sopranos, with Tony at the helm,
A mobster's life, in a turbulent realm.

Behold The Office, a mockumentary of note,
Where the mundane and the zany, in harmony, do float,
And Stranger Things, a nostalgic thrill ride,
In a world of monsters, where heroes reside.

Next, we have Seinfeld, a show about nothing,
Yet, in that very nothingness, we find something,
And Lost, a mystery, an island bizarre,
A labyrinth of secrets, near and afar.

Twin Peaks, that surreal town of Lynchian flair,
With coffee and doughnuts, and secrets in the air,
And The Wire, a gritty, unflinching tale,
Of life in Baltimore, where justice may fail.

Then, let's not forget, the supernatural charms,
Of The X-Files, with Mulder and Scully in arms,
And Westworld, a sci-fi realm, both dark and twisted,
Where the line between human and android is blistered.

Now, enter Mad Men, with slick Don Draper,
An ad man's world, filled with cunning and vapor,
And The Walking Dead, where zombies do roam,
In a post-apocalyptic land, a nightmarish home.

Witness The Big Bang Theory, where nerds unite,
In a sitcom of quirkiness, and laughter's bright light,
And Grey's Anatomy, in hospital halls,
The drama of life and death, within these walls.

Next, the political intrigue of House of Cards,
A ruthless climb to power, breaking all guards,
And Parks and Recreation, with the indomitable Leslie,
A small-town journey, full of wit and fancy.

And so, we salute, these famed TV tales,
The series that enchant us, and never grow stale,
In affectionate reverence, we honor their fame,
As the shining beacons, of America's small screen game.

In the frigid realm of vanity, a quest unfolds,
A self-indulgent story that never grows old,
The search for perfection, a portrait so bold,
A selfie to capture, a moment to be sold.

Through glass screens, our desperate eyes peer,
In search of validation, we all hold so dear,
The angle, the lighting, each strand of our hair,
As if perfect selfies could vanquish despair.

In the icy mirror, a thousand faces we seek,
A fruitless endeavor, our emotions turn bleak,
Yet onward we march, filters aplenty to wield,
In a frosty pursuit, to which we'll never yield.

As the wintry winds howl, we're lured by the glow,
Of screens that keep us captive, our hearts feeling low,
With fingers that tremble, we edit and tweak,
The depth of our emptiness, we dare not to speak.

The frost of obsession, it clings to our minds,

As we chase after shadows, and the warmth we can't find,

We're lost in the blizzard, our hearts turn to ice,

Capturing the image, we pay a steep price.

Through the frigid abyss, we're caught in a trance,

To the maddening rhythm of this chilling dance,

The pursuit of the perfect, a fantasy's embrace,

Leaving us cold and hollow, in a never-ending race.

The never-ending quest, the perfect selfie to seize,

In the cold, hollow chase, our souls forever freeze.

In the vast frozen wasteland, our hearts lay bare,

As we wander and wonder, is there warmth anywhere?

THE BLISSFUL IGNORANCE OF CLIMATE CHANGE

Yo, peeps, check it out, ain't it wild,
How we just kick back, ignoring what's defiled,
The Earth's getting warmer, we're all like "whatevs,"
As icebergs be melting, and polar bears leave.

The sea levels rise, but hey, we don't care,
Just pass me a cold one, and chill in my chair,
The storms, they be raging, but we're in our bubble,
No need to stress out or get in a kerfuffle.

Oceans polluted, the forests ablaze,
But we're too busy scrolling, in a mindless daze,
Let's post another meme, and share one more laugh,
While Mother Nature suffers, and we ignore her wrath.

So, party on, folks, 'cause ignorance is bliss,
While our planet keeps changing, and we just dismiss,
The signs all around us, the urgent alarms,
But hey, we're too cool to give in to those charms.

THE BELOVED PUMPKIN SPICE LATTE

Oh, Pumpkin Spice Latte, thou art truly dear,
A symbol of fall, consumerism's puppeteer.
A sip of thy warmth and all reason disappears,
Blinded by marketing, the masses cheer.

Once a humble gourd, now an icon of our age,
Starbucks, thy master, hath written thy page.
We flock to thy call, the frenzy is clear,
For thy sweet, spiced nectar, we blindly adhere.

What once was a harvest, a symbol of life,
Now serves as a backdrop for Instagram's strife.
We worship thy image, forgetting the truth,
A seasonal beverage, exploiting our youth.

So raise thy cup high, oh lovers of trend,
The illusion of joy that your dollars will send.
For deep in the shadows of thy frothy embrace,
Lies the shallow pursuit of a moment's embrace.

THE ADVENTURES OF DATING APPS

In a land of swiping left and right,
Tinder-ella searched for love each night.
A modern tale of romance we tell,
The dating app world, a superficial hell.

Her profile, a beacon of filters and lies,
Hoping for a match, a prince in disguise.
Amid the shirtless selfies and pick-up lines,
She held out for a spark, a love that shines.

But alas, her suitors were less than grand,
With empty words and desires so bland.
Their promises of love, like sand through her hand,
In this digital kingdom, no true love to be fanned.

The hours she wasted, the suitors dismissed,
A never-ending cycle, in which she persist.
Her heart grew heavy, her spirit wore thin,
The quest for true love, a game she can't win.

Oh Tinder-ella, your story we share,
The endless pursuit of a love so rare.
A lesson we learn from this fruitless endeavor,
In the age of dating apps, love's lost forever.

THE GRAND ILLUSION OF THE AMERICAN DREAM

In a land where dreams and aspirations reign,
The American Dream, an illusion ingrained.
A promise of wealth, success, and fame,
Yet for most, a cruel, unattainable game.

They say with hard work, you'll surely succeed,
But the truth is far darker, a deceptive creed.
For the rich grow richer, the poor struggle on,
And the grand illusion, perpetually drawn.

A white picket fence, a house so grand,
A tale of prosperity in a flourishing land.
But beneath the surface, the reality's grim,
A system rigged, where the chances are slim.

The dream is a myth, a tale we uphold,
As we chase after fortune, our souls bought and sold.
In the end, we're left with a bitter taste,
The American Dream, an illusion we chased.

For in this land of dreams, it's easy to see,

The grand illusion is but a fallacy.

The pursuit of happiness, a tale we're sold,

As we cling to the mirage, our dreams left untold.

In the city of angels, where lights flicker and glow,
A dynasty reigns, a spectacle, a show.
The Kardashians, a clan we can't comprehend,
A magnificent enigma, a peculiar trend.

With cameras flashin', and followers amassed,
Their lives on display, a relentless broadcast.
But what do they offer, these icons so grand?
A tale of vanity, a thirst we can't withstand.

From selfie to selfie, and scandal to feud,
Their drama unfolds, and we're all unglued.
We watch as they conquer the realm of fame,
Their lives our obsession, a puzzling game.

But why do we care, what do they give,
These enigmatic figures, who live to relive?
Perhaps they're a mirror, a reflection of our own,
An urban desire, a hunger that's grown.

In a world of facades and material strife,

The Kardashians embody the modern urban life.

A magnificent enigma, a question we pose,

As we chase their allure, our fascination grows.

Oh, the standards of beauty, impossibly high,
In a world obsessed with the perfect thigh.
We chase and we strive, for a dream that's a lie,
A mirage that eludes us, as we try and try.

Photoshop queens and picture-perfect kings,
Selling a fantasy, as reality stings.
Our self-worth distorted, by airbrushed extremes,
No room for the real, in these pixel-perfect schemes.

The billboards and magazines, they whisper and shout,
"Be thinner, be taller, or you'll be left out!"
But as we chase shadows, we fail to see,
The beauty within us, uniquely set free.

We strive to conform, to fit in their mold,
As the truth of our essence is left untold.
The impossibly high standards, a cage we create,
To stifle our spirits, to suffocate.

So, let's break the chains, reject the deceit,

And embrace our own beauty, both bitter and sweet.

For the standards they set, are not what we need,

To love and accept, our true selves, indeed.

Ah, the art of stalking, a subtle affair,
On the platforms of social, where we pretend not to care.
We scroll and we swipe, with a sly little grin,
As we peer into lives, we're not meant to be in.

We judge and we gossip, in whispers so slight,
As we scrutinize others, from morning till night.
Anonymously lurking, in this digital game,
We all play our part, in the masquerade of shame.

The subtlety of stalking, a skill we've refined,
In the depths of our screens, where we're lost and confined.
Comparing our lives, to the highlight reels,
As we ignore the ache, that loneliness reveals.

We laugh at their missteps, and envy their wins,
But forget the battles, that lie deep within.
For the screens that we stalk, they only conceal,
The truest of struggles, that no filter reveals.

So, let us ponder, as we play this charade,
The subtle intrusion, of the stalking brigade.
For the lives that we covet, and the envy we sow,
Are merely illusions, of a grand puppet show.

In the land of gadgets, where tech does abound,
A curious phenomenon is often found.
The masses assembled, with cash in their hands,
For the latest device, that the market commands.

The newest iPhone, they all yearn to possess,
For how could they live with a model that's less?
The features, the colors, a triumph of style,
Surely, owning this phone must be worth every mile.

They camp out in lines, with a gleam in their eyes,
The anticipation of purchase, their ultimate prize.
As they enter the store, they can't help but feel glee,
At the thought of that Apple, so shiny and wee.

And once in their grasp, they feel such elation,
The envy of friends, instant social fixation.
But alas, in the shadows, a secret does lie,
For the cycle continues, as time passes by.

The irony lies in this fervent pursuit,

Of a phone that's replaced, in a blink, absolute.

Yet the masses return, with their wallets held high,

In a quest for the latest, to conquer and buy.

So, let us reflect on this ceaseless desire,

To possess the newest, a game ever dire.

For in the end, we may find, as we make our selection,

That the joy of the chase, far exceeds its connection.

The All-Encompassing Fear of Being Uncool

Oh, woe to the souls who dread being uncool,
Who yearn to fit in, like a cog in a school.
A fear so consuming, it shakes to the core,
For in the great game of life, it's the ultimate chore.

To dress in the latest, to speak the right slang,
A never-ending battle, a societal twang.
For who could endure the unbearable plight,
Of being the one who's not shining so bright?

We chase after trends, like a moth to a flame,
In hopes that our peers will remember our name.
But the irony lies in this desperate race,
For uniqueness we shun, as we strive to keep pace.

To be cool or uncool, is that really the measure,
Of a life full of joy, or a soul full of treasure?
For in truth, what is cool, but a fleeting illusion,
A mirage that dissolves, amidst all the confusion?

Let's shed this façade and embrace who we are,

For in life's grand design, we're each a bright star.

The fear of being uncool, we must put to rest,

For in our own skin, we are truly our best.

Oh, the meme, that tiny morsel of internet delight,
A digital delight that captures our attention, day and night.
It's humor and it's wisdom, encapsulated in a frame,
A window to our zeitgeist, a reflection of our game.

From cat to dog, from frog to gnome, they all have had their time,
A fleeting moment in the spotlight, then replaced by the next sublime.
For who can resist the meme's allure, its simplicity and its charm,
A moment of laughter in the chaos, an antidote to harm.

How ironic that these pixels, these bites of internet fare,
Can inspire a sense of unity, as if we're all quite rare.
In truth, they are but mirrors, reflecting our collective soul,
The laughter and the tears, the stories left untold.

And yet, we can't deny it, the power that memes hold,
Their ability to transcend borders, to bring warmth to the cold.
So let us raise our glasses, in a toast to these digital treats,
For in a world of chaos, they offer us a moment of sweet retreat.

THE UNFATHOMABLE MYSTERY OF MISSING SOCKS

Ah, the mystery of missing socks, a conundrum so profound,
A puzzle that perplexes us, as we search and look around.
Where do these foot-warmers go, when they vanish from our sight?
Do they slip into a secret realm, a world of endless night?

With every load of laundry, the numbers seem to grow,
A solitary sock remains, its partner's fate unknown.
Is there a hidden vortex, where these lonely socks convene?
A land of mismatched stockings, where they plot and scheme?

Or perhaps there is a creature, dwelling in the deep,
A monster made of lint and fluff, on lost socks does it feed.
It lies in wait, a patient hunter, biding its sweet time,
And when the moment's right, it strikes, a crime most sublime.

Oh, the cynicism of it all, the utter absurdity,
To ponder on the whereabouts of our missing accessories.
For in a world of chaos, of pain and endless strife,
We fixate on the mundane, the trivialities of life.

So let us laugh and shake our heads, at this great cosmic joke,
The unsolvable enigma, of the socks that simply spoke:
"Goodbye, dear human, I've had enough, my purpose has been served,
I leave you now, to ponder on, the fate that I deserved."

THE QUIET DESPERATION OF UNANSWERED DMS

Ah, the void of unanswered DMs, a place where hopes are shattered,
A graveyard of digital whispers, where dreams and ego battered.
You slide into their inbox, with words so smooth and sly,
Yet silence greets you coldly, as hours and days slip by.

The quiet desperation builds, as you ponder your approach,
Did you come on too strong, or were you just a momentary roach?
The messages left on 'read,' an unrelenting reminder,
Of a conversation halted, like a flame devoid of tinder.

Perhaps, just maybe, it's a game of cat and mouse,
A dance of digital courtship, confined to this virtual house.
You wait and wonder, "Will they ever write me back?"
A question left unanswered, like a train derailed from its track.

And yet, in this ironic twist, you start to see the light,
For isn't life much richer than the pixels in our sight?
Unanswered DMs, like leaves, may wither and fall,
But true connection lies beyond, just beyond that virtual wall.

Embrace the quiet desperation, let it fuel your inner fire,

For in the grander scheme of things, your worth is so much higher.

Unanswered DMs may sting, like a slap across the face,

But in the end, we'll find our way, beyond this cyberspace.

THE STRUGGLES OF THE URBAN HIPSTER

In the concrete jungle where the hipsters dwell,
A tale of beards, craft beer, and vintage wear, I'll tell.
With their fixie bikes and mason jars, they navigate the scene,
A world of kale and quinoa, where avocado's green.

They hunt for vinyl records in thrift stores near and far,
Dreaming of that perfect find, a rare and ancient star.
From morning's cold brew coffee, to the evenings spent at dives,
Their lives a quest for authenticity, a hipster's dream contrived.

On weekends, they convene at trendy rooftop bars,
Sipping on artisanal cocktails, beneath the urban stars.
Their conversations deep and cultured, for they know it all,
Discussing politics and art, they stand aloof and tall.

The urban hipster's struggle, a plight so bittersweet,
A paradox of longing, for a life both cool and neat.
They shun the mainstream culture, yet yearn to find their place,
In a world that keeps on turning, at an ever-faster pace.

So let us laugh and celebrate, the hipster's wild endeavor,
For in their quest for meaning, they bring humor and much pleasure.
And though they may be judged or mocked, for their peculiar ways,
Their journey is a testament, to the spirit of our days.

THE DIVINE COMEDY OF COLLEGE REJECTION LETTERS

In the halls of academia, where dreams and futures intertwine,
A tale unfolds, a comedy, of college rejections and their sign.
For 'tis a story bittersweet, of students young and bright,
Who face the crushing blow of fate, their dreams to take flight.

Armed with essays, scores, and grades, they enter the fray,
Hoping to find acceptance in the halls where knowledge lay.
But lo! The letters come, with form and cruel precision,
Their prose a dagger to the heart, a cold and harsh decision.

"Dear Applicant," they all begin, a phrase so trite and terse,
"We regret to inform you," follows, the opening of the curse.
With feigned sympathy, they write, of the competitive lot,
A veiled insult to the wounded, a reminder of the battles fought.

The parents' wails, the students' tears, a chorus of despair,
As rejection letters pile on desks, a burden they must bear.
Yet in this cruel comedy, a truth does lie within,
A lesson to be learned, amidst the chaos and the din.

For college rejections sting, a temporary pain,

But life is vast and varied, with countless paths to gain.

So laugh at the divine comedy, of the letters filled with sorrow,

And know that in the darkest night, the sun will rise tomorrow.

THE THRILLING SUSPENSE OF WAITING FOR THE UBER

The thrilling suspense, the mounting anticipation,
As we wait for the Uber, our modern transportation.
The app on our screens, with the map, oh so bright,
The car icon moves closer, promising respite.

But lo! What is this? A sudden detour ensues,
Our driver is lost, in a maze of avenues.
The ETA shifts, from two minutes to ten,
Our patience grows thin, as we wait once again.

We glance at our phones, the blue dot stands alone,
As the car spins in circles, in a dance all its own.
The minutes crawl by, with a snail's sluggish pace,
We wonder if walking might have won the race.

A sigh of despair, as we check the app once more,
The icon now stationary, a block from our door.
We ponder the fate of our ride yet to come,
The thrilling suspense, now a dull hum.

In this modern age, where convenience is king,
The waiting game teases, a cruel and mocking sting.
For the Uber that tarries, a lesson it imparts,
That life is uncertain, and the journey's just the start.

In the realm of caffeine, where corporate giants rule,
There's a game being played, and we're merely the fools.
Starbucks, the titan, its green siren calls,
Beneath the facade, its loyalty app stalls.

Oh, the highs and the lows, the rewards we adore,
A free drink, a cookie, we crave even more.
We spend and we swipe, the cycle's unending,
Our devotion unwavering, our dollars unspending.

But the lows, they do haunt us, as we sip our cold brew,
The price of our loyalty, the cost overdue.
The overpriced lattes, the taste of defeat,
We've sold our souls for a sugary treat.

The app buzzes brightly, "Just one more star,"
We take the bait, pay the price, and we're back at the bar.
The siren, she grins, her trap has been laid,
In this game of Starbucks loyalty, we've all been played.

For in this world of caffeine, where Starbucks reigns supreme,
Our loyalty is purchased, with a frothy, sweet dream.
And though we may grumble, with each sip we concede,
To the highs and the lows, the Starbucks siren, we heed.

THE ENCHANTING WORLD OF YOGA PANTS

In the land of stretchy fabric, where vanity lies,
The yoga pants emerge, a captivating prize.
A form-fitting marvel, a siren's sweet song,
Drawing us in, as we blindly play along.

Arousing envy and awe, on each passerby,
The yoga pants whisper, "Come, give us a try."
We heed their sweet call, and part with our cash,
In hopes that our leggings will make us less brash.

But the enchantment, it fades, as reality looms,
We're not magically transformed, in our spandex cocoons.
For in truth, the pants promise much more than they give,
As we're lured into thinking they'll change how we live.

In gyms and in cafes, in malls and on streets,
The yoga pants' presence, our vision, it greets.
But though we may hope for a life-changing quest,
In our snug-fitting leggings, we're merely well-dressed.

So, listen, dear friend, to the lesson I share,

The enchanting world of yoga pants, best approached with great care.

For the comfort they offer, and the style they possess,

Are but simple illusions, a fashionista's false test.

In the cavernous realm where cardboard prevails,
An Amazon package embarks on its tale.
From warehouse to doorstep, its journey unfolds,
A tale that seems grand, yet in truth, we've been sold.

It starts with a click, a consumer's desire,
The hunger for things we believe we require.
Wrapped in ambition, with tape as its bind,
The package sets forth, seeking hearts it may find.

Through trucks, planes, and hands, it traverses with speed,
A testament to commerce and unbridled greed.
A race to the finish, a desperate attempt,
To satisfy yearnings, consumer contempt.

Arriving at last, at the threshold it waits,
Anticipation surging, to seal its grand fate.
But as doors open wide, and hands clutch in glee,
The package, once cherished, loses its decree.

Torn open and scattered, its contents revealed,
The Amazon package, its destiny sealed.
Its journey, so thrilling, now nothing but waste,
As the grandeur it promised, was naught but a taste.

So heed this cold tale, of the Amazon quest,
For the sublime journey, is but a jest.
As we chase after things, in cardboard disguise,
The truth lies obscured, by consumerist lies.

THE TRAGIC KINGDOM OF INFLUENCER CULTURE

Behold the kingdom, where vanity reigns,
A realm of illusion, where ego sustains.
The Tragic Kingdom, a place all adore,
Influencer culture, where truth's but a bore.

Through filters and angles, they craft their façade,
With likes and with comments, their power unmarred.
In a world built on falsehoods, their faces well-known,
These sovereigns of cyberspace, their kingdoms have grown.

A sea of endorsements, and products to share,
A life full of glamour, no burden to bear.
But beneath the surface, where shadows reside,
A darker reality, the influencers hide.

In the pursuit of perfection, their sanity bends,
As they chase validation, the madness descends.
For the kingdom they built, on quicksand it stands,
The weight of the crown, slips through trembling hands.

As followers gather, and subjects admire,
The influencers falter, their souls growing tired.
For the Tragic Kingdom, where lies are the key,
Is a kingdom of emptiness, where no one is free.

So. heed the grim tale, of this digital land,
And question the culture, that we've let expand.
For in chasing the fame, and the fortune it brings,
We've lost sight of truth, and the joy life can sing.

The Odyssey of Online Shopping

In the realm of digital vastness, a shopper's quest begins,
A journey fraught with choices, where temptation always wins.
With fingertips at ready, and a credit card in hand,
They navigate the maze of deals that stretch across the land.

From Amazon to eBay, and the sites one can't pronounce,
The odyssey of online shopping, with every click, surmounts.
The cart fills up with trinkets, clothes, and gadgets of all kinds,
As ads allure and discounts sway the unsuspecting minds.

A sweater here, some shoes right there, a blender for the kitchen,
Our valiant shopper's fingers dance, bewitched by sales bewitchin'.
Yet in the midst of retail glee, the shipping fees appear,
A daunting foe, a bitter pill, to darken shopping cheer.

But fear not, oh brave shopper, for a triumph lies ahead,
With promo codes and memberships, the shipping costs are shed.
The checkout now approaches, and the end is drawing near,
A final click, the order placed, a sigh of sweet relief.

And so concludes the odyssey of online shopping's tale,
Where patience, wit, and fortitude in equal parts prevail.
But rest not long, my weary friend, for soon you'll hear the call,
Of Cyber Monday's siren song, and once more, you will fall.

THE UNBEARABLE WEIGHT OF EXISTENTIAL DREAD

Oh, the weight of existential dread, a burden we all bear,
When pondering life's mysteries, in moments of despair.
But let's not fret and furrow brows, for humor lies within,
The cosmic joke of consciousness, that makes us laugh and grin.

We question why we're here at all, a speck amidst the stars,
As we go about our daily grind, commuting in our cars.
The meaning of life's grand design, a puzzle none can solve,
Yet still, we search and contemplate, our minds forever rove.

We grapple with mortality, the finite time we've got,
And sometimes in the darkest hours, our thoughts become distraught.
But there's a bright side to this mess, an irony, I swear,
The certainty of nothingness, we all must come to bear.

So let us laugh at our demise, the chaos of it all,
The randomness of fate and chance, that leaves us in its thrall.
For though the weight of dread is great, we have a choice, you see,
To face the void with laughter, and embrace absurdity.

THE DELIGHTS OF A FAILED DIET

Oh, the sweet delights of a failed diet, a tale we all know well,
The siren call of cookies, cakes, and donuts, we can't quell.
With resolutions made in earnest, determined to succeed,
We bravely face the grocery aisles, with healthy food to feed.

But lo and behold, temptation's there, with sugar-laden treats,
Their colors bright, their smells divine, they beckon us to eat.
We try to keep our willpower, our courage held up high,
But in the end, resistance wanes, and to our cravings, we comply.

We rationalize with twisted thoughts, a cheat day won't be bad,
And so we scarf down chocolate bars, and tell ourselves we're glad.
The diet's dream, now but a joke, as we indulge once more,
In candy, chips, and ice cream cones, like kids inside a store.

We may lament our lack of strength, our figures growing round,
Yet still, we find a morsel of joy, in the treats that we have found.
For life's too short for deprivation, a balance we must seek,
To savor sweets and scrumptious bites, while still remaining meek.

So let us raise a toast to failed diets, their lessons and their charms,
A reminder that our appetites, can sometimes cause us harm.
But in the end, we'll find our stride, and moderation's key,
To enjoy life's tasty pleasures, while maintaining sanity.

In the age of endless scrolling, where perfection seems the goal,
The struggle of choosing filters plagues each and every soul.
We snap our selfies, food, and pets, with hope to share and please,
But faced with countless options, we're brought down to our knees.

Oh Valencia, Clarendon, or Ludwig, which to choose?
Each filter casts a different light, a battle we must lose.
X-Pro II brings out the dark, while Crema lightens up,
And when we find the perfect one, we feel like we've won the cup.

We swipe through options, left and right, with fingers swift and keen,
Adjusting brightness, contrast too, ensuring the perfect sheen.
The minutes turn to hours long, as we perfect our art,
Forgetting that the world outside, continues on its part.

At last, the choice is made, our masterpiece complete,
And yet, we sit in silence, as our doubt begins to seep.
"Will they like it, will they care? Have I made the perfect choice?"
A cacophony of questions, an overwhelming noise.

The struggle of choosing filters, a battle that we wage,

A symbol of our times, where likes and hearts are all the rage.

But as we face this arduous task, let's not forget the truth,

That life's not measured by our filters, but by the joy of our youth.

The Paradox of Modern Loneliness

In the age of digital companions, where we're never quite alone,
A paradox emerges, one that's chilling to the bone.
Always "connected," our screens held close, our friends at fingertips,
And yet we find ourselves adrift, as loneliness tightly grips.

We swipe and tap and click away, in search of love or laughter,
But do we find the solace sought, or is it just disaster?
We slide into DMs, send out snaps, our tweets dispersed like birds,
But often find the silence back, a void that's undeterred.

Oh, modern loneliness, you've got us in your snare,
In a world where virtual friendships thrive, it simply isn't fair.
We've traded smiles and handshakes for emojis in a row,
And while we gain convenience, we lose the warmth we used to know.

Our screens glow bright as day turns night, our eyes not getting rest,
We search for validation, hoping someone thinks we're best.
But as the hours slip away, and the night turns into day,
We realize our own plight, in this paradox we lay.

In the end, we sit and ponder, wondering where we've erred,
For modern loneliness has struck, a fate we never dared.
No moral here, no lesson learned, just laughter to be had,
For in this digital age, it seems, the joke's on us, my lad.

THE CURIOUS CASE OF THE VANISHING PRIVACY

Gather 'round, dear listeners, for a tale I wish to tell,
Of privacy's demise, a once great thing that sadly fell.
In days of yore, our secrets kept, our lives lived far apart,
But now we dwell in glass-like homes, and share each beating heart.

Facebook, Twitter, Instagram, and more, they seem so kind,
A never-ending quest to learn what thoughts lurk in our minds.
We feed them all our data, our dreams, desires, and fears,
And in return, they give us memes and ads for trendy gears.

The vanishing of privacy, a magic trick supreme,
As we reveal our inner selves for all the world to glean.
We've traded solitude for likes, our dignity for shares,
The notion of a private life, it seems, no one now cares.

Ah, dear privacy, once held so close, now tossed aside like trash,
We've sold you for convenience and a little extra cash.
And now we stand, exposed and bare, our lives an open book,
The world peering in, a hungry gaze, a collective, eager look.

So, join me in a toast, my friends, to the privacy of old,

To the time when lives were quiet, and secrets could be told.

For in this age of oversharing and the endless thirst for fame,

The vanishing of privacy is the price we pay for the game.

THE DELICATE ART OF TEXTING BACK

The subtle dance of texting back, a waltz we all partake,
The thrill of typing, backspacing, as our fragile hearts do quake.
To answer or ignore, my friends, that is the question here,
The stakes are high, the timing tight, a world of angst and fear.

We labor over every word, each emoji we consider,
Do I dare send that winky face? Will it make them think I'm bitter?
The bubbles rise, then disappear, a cruel game we play,
The agony of waiting, as seconds turn to days.

Our minds consumed, the guessing game, deciphering their tone,
A single "lol" or "haha," leaves us feeling all alone.
Is it just a simple joke, or layered with disdain?
We read between the lines, and yet, confusion does remain.

The rules unwritten, tacit codes, to navigate this maze,
A labyrinth of digital talk, our thumbs now set ablaze.
In days of yore, a face-to-face, the clarity of speech,
But now we dwell in pixel land, with perfect prose to reach.

The delicate art of texting back, a skill we must all hone,
For in the age of screens and swipes, we're never quite alone.
Our words immortalized in blue or green, to be reviewed,
A chronicle of human strife, the language misconstrued.